SANNYASIN

Jordan Cambridge

TABLE OF CONTENTS

Hydrogen Thoughts

The erudite, cramming, brains like a ramshackle attic.
If it is important, I won't have to remember,
I'll have to act.
The course
of life, reincarnating in epiphanies.
Mind is reborn again, and again
into infinity.
The story of the joyful
human
is dead by age twenty.
Your story is not made
for happiness; but for adventure.

Excitedly targeting the light, the blind destination of the mind.
Without dedication to the heart,
they are stranded inside
the shadows of passion.

The disorientated creed of self-realisation, slapped on road signs:
inviting you into the wing-clipped arms of heaven.
Admit, that overdosing on drugs, is suicide.

The flightless, stone path of hope
has nowhere to rest.
The relentless, truthful, self knows,
peace comes from focus.

The sightless iron-minded built
the joyful scaffolds of paradise.
Remember, the Utopia idea
came from the Spartans,
who had no use
for unarmed dreamers.

*Our castle of reality was lost in the wars of
late childhood.
The oldest trees, are weak shields against the city.
From park to park, an anxious exile.*

*To everyone I am a vagabond with my rag of truth.
It warms me in my moon-bound dreams where imagination,
and reality
are one consciousness.*

*We have isolated the infinite in humanity,
and rampage in wrathful highs
of the hero.
A guiding principle is needed
to navigate
who you are
in the world that simply, is.*

*Secluded leaves of the spirit, flourish upward on many branches.
Blinding light finds the sun-painted flowers of the universe.
Any religion you create must be indestructible:
Don't copy and paste.*

*You raised your banner of knowledge, charged with
stone-shattering intention, laid low in destiny's swordplay.
Turn your detention into a gym:
Push up and down,
lift, and let go.*

*In histories of order, you have lost the way.
Pathfinder, listen to each whispering
of the divine.
What are your feelings teaching you?
Be ordained in the arms of love.*

*Starlight prince of the beloved.
Do not reside in the delightful destinations of darkness.
The wistful drugs of god.
Thinking we are, who we are,
is how the universe hallucinates.*

Being a human is good, but apex predators die.
Tangles of thorny spirits;
What we do effects everyone else,
and they'll always be pain.
Might as well go forward.

Look into the waters of enquiry.
I won't get away with hubris.
The shimmering lights of knowledge, tell of a galaxy filled with hope.
I am born of love, so why did I do this?

The wrathfully ambitious walk the lines of power.
Watch yourself seek superiority;
The golden trumpet fantasies of coronation
for being different.

From the cold iron devotion to the smouldering oak fires of apathy.
Death, an empty cauldron, suspended.
The living, of life
is between breaths.

The Dark Wanderer (Trapped Between Worlds)

My first thought every morning:
"I am alone."

The rage in the void, fathering bastard thoughts.
I focus on things,
one at a time.

My tired soul finally wilts, and suddenly blooms.
I have a consciousness
behind all of this.

My brain, like a fiery tree of knowing.
Certainty burns in me;
An artist, a mystic, a warrior.

I pass dark towers of order, marred by claw marks and footholds.
Is it equality if you match the standards set by oppressors?

My feet fail on the path.
Imagination, despairing wings, carrying me to peace.
"Would this matter, if I were a dragon?"

I am ravenous;
Nerves seeking feeling,
bursting from my carrion host.
I am told I'm too fast, too extreme.
But this life is a lesson;
How much time do you think we have?

I stand on the rocks of chaos.
Human nature should be embraced,
and transcended.
The golden armour gloried,
among the lustful beasts.
Those who do not discipline themselves,
become farm animals, saddled, and broken
by patient men.

Our blazing souls rule all of us as kings, refusing to snuff our lives'
passions.
Nonattachment doesn't mean giving up;
Just stepping out, going back to play.

The scaffold of illusion must be struck away.
Food cannot be enjoyed by the starving,
the lonely; their friends,
drunks; the parties.

The spears of inspiration must draw blood.
Meet them with might.
You must die for them.
Asleep, you cannot live your dreams.

My faith sheds its
golden armour glory.
My lion-hearted cloak of rage.
Humanity is at dusk.
I feel the call,
I must transcend.
I fear that song of the dark.
To be a heartless,
mindful husk.
Trapped between worlds.

Newcomer

I am a shattered seeker.
I look for signs everywhere, bored of devils with feathered wings.

Do not chide my bleeding, dead pragmatism.
I hate what I see
because I long to see more.

The uncaring path of justice does not nourish me.
We are not a Tupperware of consciousness,
we are glasses of water, dropped into the sea.

In a towel, I hold myself as a child, salve my red skinned destruction.
There is no finish line,
no true end to struggles.

I dream of golden sands, and you, the queen of angels.
When I don't know what I am,
I serve you.

I see jewels in stone natures and let them be.
Every visitor is a manifestation.
There is no arrogance.
With me, I am the king of knowing.
There is no such thing as an essential me.

The eagle empires are forged by millions.
Your soul will find it's way back.
Life dissipates with the steam of your cup.
Your output is the greatness
your team achieves.

The Retreat

You are tired from carrying your intention.
These shouldered milestones are holding you back.
Reduce the borders of your kingdom.
Battle weary palace, carpets, trodden and dusty
from marching orders.
Attack until it is dealt with.
Never use the word "should";
why shackle yourself?

Your truth does not weigh anything
to the bitter conjuring of fate.
Guilt just is an insight:
Holding the bar too high,
jurors of hate in your mind.

You question the sun's debt
in the tree's fruit.
How does nature know perfection?
The apple did not grant knowledge,
it gave us power to manifest.
It is supposed to go wrong,
we are God, just practicing.

The dreaded halls
of the mind stretch endlessly.
What should I do today?
Whatever I feel like.

I draw on my hollowed warrior spirit.
So far down, through the bottom.
I am in a free fall,
unbound to the earth.

These are the courageous highs of poetry.

Sharded Valleys

Bestial slacker, that is in fact, a knowing one.
If I make time to do something,
I must make time to finish it.

We are barbarians, woven into being civilised.
No one will warm themselves with it
in dark nights.
Love should be lived as if it's days were numbered.

Death, over me like a dreadful guardian;
Gutters, on the path, bringing comfort to my wayward stress.
I do not know how many incarnations I have left.

The taste of joy brings an onslaught of an egoic soul.
Fire, burning every opportunity it finds.
I bellow candlelight softly, cross legged, and lazy, finding my inner
sunshine.

Dizzy, hopeless, miscreants.
The bored,
look on a river,
without sailing it.
Water flows in all pathways.
It erodes, with the knowledge
that all things are impermeant.

Watch the moon's silver face, turn from you.
Move and act quickly to not be outpaced.
At the point it next peaks,
speak what you have learned.

The masters of the earth survive on painful nectar.
They journey in desolation.
Happiness, a process of eliminating
the chains of their attention.

The wisdom of nature guides me
to the ancient ways I'm losing.
Discipline, freeing me from the chains
of pointless choosing.

With our heads in the clouds,
we are the serfs of heavenly fathers.
Since the beginning, whole lives are made of words.
The point of all stories
is a lesson.

We clash and spit like lava.
Boundless incarnations of soulfire, interacting.
Only the wounded are truly wise.
Sit with me brother, we'll bleed out together.
Side by side regardless of colours.

Life is boring to the philosopher.
The clawing self-battles in shoulder bumping crowds of grey.
I know all about this pain.
Remain silent,
no one listens anyway.

The rising war of humanity, growing bolder, as the stewards of the
universe.
The brighter the light, the darker the shadow.
That is why I am here.

A ghostly traveller; a peaceful visitor to this plain.
Higher than the hollow whispers of legend.
I guard the island of my soul from demons.

Dream

Your brain is a lazy seeker of the spiritual.
My grim sabre slices the cerebral
I am you, merely filtered through
a different existence.

I am a warrior of the desolate spirit world.
My mind has no direction, boundless like the clouds of galaxies.
The electric bolts leap about,
refusing capture to a blank page.

A tranquil vagabond, or lord of the earth.
The words you voice,
is the universe itself.
Carry the story with wise choices.

Crying in the golden plains of freedom.
To know the ethereal weave of reality in your hands.
A spiritual battle, a shamanic dance, ascending beyond dead gods and
benign demons.

This is a dream,
in the right point of view.
Hold lucidity when you can.
Your island of intuition, sacrificed
in fires of goliath plans
and empty legends.
You can't live your dream life
if you don't realise
you're dreaming.

Imperial sun rising over heathen night.
I think of you each morning.
your warmth carries through
the dreamy walls
made in your heart.

Your light streaks over the hills.
Winter breath and furred hood, I
depart on my holy travels,
with a will to meet you.

To find this forgone thing
in minds eye.
The words of past and present bind thee.
Words that weave the world
held by tree named Yggdrasil.
Shapes and sounds
combine like hammer and anvil
forging fate.
Our fates cooling from fleeing winters,
holds our shape once made to purpose.
I have read you, wise ones,
you are rebirthed in me.
A column of seekers cobbling a road.
I walk ever closer to my foresight.

Paracosmicon Gate

*The serene ripples of sacrament flew
towards the strands my mind,
along pink clouds
and sunshine,
blue like it's underwater.*

*Floating, in the nectar, from elves
kind enough to share with me.
On a beach with
red sand and a green sea.*

*I think of the bright moon-howlers,
the whole galaxy of them out there.
I like to think I'm staring at them.
Our imaginations not
close enough to meet.*

*From the war-like khans,
to the hidden ones,
stealing crumbs and headphones from our sofas, to the weary lords, and
dragons.
Jazzed, on the mead of joy, the foolhardy sage.
These old ones look on, grim demons, living in an ocean of problems.*

*I wander among them, gleefully, pen pouring lines.
Compassion summoned, as I imagine
a wise one, or sorcerer, wearing lavender to guide me.
Down in the swamps, for herbs to makes drinks.
Meet the down to earth, dwarves of the southern sea cliffs.
Beer mixed with salt and tofurky spits.
All these crazy threads of faith and lies
weaved
by valiant sprites, meddling with the fabric of space-time.*

Giamind

The starry night opens
a bright cavern of power.
Thousand suns reaching outward.
Stretching mind, for a moment
I taste ecstasy,
the delicate magic at work.
Flying on bound on lines of determination.
The rash sages, worship them
as our fates.
Just as we see the future
in babies,
unmade by parents.

The ecstatic wine of the soul from
the night's sky.
The celestial fluid,
dark emptiness, jewelled with
twinkling innocence.
Earth, a scarred journeyman in the cosmos,
drunk on life, forgets itself.
The wispy clouds of consciousness
turned to mad waring kings.

The world spirit dances and forgets its body.
Whirling in a cloak of gallant stars.
The barren planets don't judge.
The threads of fate are cut
by jagged actualisation.
Rotating just as before,
but so alive.

Rune speaker
Seated like a mountain.
centred, iron veined,
the mead of gods,
made teachings of fate.

I will speak to every
idle man's heart.
See darkness flee at
sunlight cracks.
Mead, mulled, made
molten thoughts.
Welding sounds, my
weapon forged.
My Words, a hammer,
My pen, a chisel.
Midgard magick,
carved by will.

Repetition

I am here, well found
sitting like a mountain
on an astounding pile
of shitty circumstances,
destiny or free will,
undecided, or unbound
by morality.

Breathing the words of artists,
my heart drums ecstasy, feeling lost
in clumsy clouds of
mortal tongues
and revelry.

One node
of the greater reflection,
inextricably connected
to the infinite
things
of this infinite
universe perpetually,
extending
across relativity.

*Already,
in my mere presence,
I have plucked the strings
of fate and luck
for each passenger
and thing on this mortal plain.
Every disgusting pig-trough
buffet.
Every utterance,
and loud shouted word
when people don't hear
what we say.
Every death hunted moment
when,
taking time,
and wasting time
seem to be the same.
Every person acting worse,
lacking inertia on their path,
hurting for a heart,
but they can't
have mine.
We're leaving school buildings,
entering workplaces, marriages,
and making babies,
forgetting to ask our parents
if we are still children.
Histories of fences and podiums filled with valiant hope whispers.
Old men and pledges of honesty,
in a world of legislation,
more complicated than promises.
Humanity, acting in certain settings
and scenes, or a single moment,
distilled through the vetting
and checking social media,
remixed with insincere motives.*

*Impurities on fewer
and fewer pixels
on tiny screens.*

*What you have seen
is clear and pure,
but it is a drop
you see,
from a vast,
deep,
and polluted
ocean.*

*Slick, quick pitch to fix it all.
Consistency is critical.
There is a bitch in habitual,
and repetition is difficult.
Pull it together
more than just atomically,
with biological and economic
fixes.
Searching for
the astonishing "rich"
that is
ritual.*

*In other words,
it's all repetition.*

The Hierophant

In the valiant fabric of leadership, you drape yourself.
Holding yourself accountable for their suffering puts you above them.

Grim faced, hidden in the oceans of others.
Present yourself as who you are becoming.

The pillars of reality, our heaven, are on clouds, floating in emptiness.
My pen blood, a sacrament made for my place in it.
The universe is playing a game with itself, and the game is love.

Come into this as something new.
A funky endgame to the demonic madness.
Having a mission is what makes you happy,
but you must show up.

The radical blades of compassion,
cut through realities blinders,
like the mystics with violet hair
you see in the streets.
What have they seen?

Beware the dark ones; The pain merchants.
Providing the serenity of pleasant debts,
a vengeful reap with each passing moon.
The bright furies of the old ones
still burns in our blood.
The neon exchanged for
a sea green.
To be a sage, in an age of cities and artifice.

I drift in the shadows.
My gleeful wonder,
like lightening in dark clouds.
Head and heart,
flashing in moments of clarity.
If you want balance, see how comfortable you are,
standing on one leg forever.
The weak hearted cotton sharks seek comfort
with beauty.
Exercise in strife.
Remind yourself how
powerful you are.

The most noble elders find themselves lost in wish vapours.
Your mind, a wild galaxy of sensation.
Thinking is one of the most joyous things you can do,
don't waste it.

Anjaanahatar

Despair,
at the masks we wear
to protect our true selves.
If you and I are one,
would you care about me?

We live in our hearts,
but forget,
so we can be held
in wonder:
Falling in love.

Suffering is how we wake up.
Forgetting again,
far saner
than remembering.

An open palm, and open eyes,
let go of painful tears,
and welcome change.

New State

Outlawing the giants trying to heal hamlets,
public sector protecting it's interests
through humanitarianism.
The vampiric collective wield judges hammers,
It is crazy to think of laws as a fortress of perfectionism.

Made with the hands of slaves,
serfs, and subjects,
but to be rectified
from the inside
with the building
still standing?
Impossible.
Crazed warriors of justice glazing
over rules of freedom.
Can rules and freedom be the same thing?

Mentions of red and blue on
screens like Cyan and Magenta.
The artificial reality of clank-labourers
besieging prized monoliths of
democracy; Networked by
isolated control towers.

*Veracious spiritual glyphs
cause glitches in the system,
with preaching,
gloats, posts, lies, reposts,
twitch and twitter.
Imprisoned behind the gates
of Maya.
The Mayans predicted this,
or the Aztecs?
shit.
I can't recall the
click-bait I bit…*

*Unified in a fog of solitude
with flying arcs of insults, like flashing fire birds,
leave behind trails of smoke, which lead
to mirrors and appearing to ourselves
as our profiles,
dictating who we are as
marketing information.*

*The wild persona of liberty cannot be classified and claimed,
named under laws,
blown away like dust
across borders.
It is the suffocating fate of those in power.
To complain, condemn, regulate what they
do not understand, expanding at a rate
that can only get away from you.*

*The tempestuous
sanctum of purpose
found in the nation state.*

The Wonder

Dreamy petals of identity grown from a universe seed,
attracting the antagonistic bombardment
of safety needs.

The fun maker's judgement
is abandoned,
to bring about the flow
of fate,
closer to our ancestors.

I am consumed by the whisper of
unity seen in
the beauty of everyday life.
The shadows of gods are in destitution,
but that is no excuse
for not having
striking visions
and furious,
insatiable, curiosity.

Quit your job.

The Dark Journey

In the abstract confinement of illusion.
It's obvious you must give up to choose.
The weary insurrectionists, rebelling against
the ideals of the ninety-eight percent
in mediocrity.

Destiny cannot be escaped.
Prison rebellions will be supressed,
until the mellow of battlefield hearts
beat slowly, in a chant for peace.

Sever the manacles of governance.
Fury is the key,
but the freedom is hollow
if you continue to identify
with the inside
of your history.

The clarity flashes like lightning,
but carry the thunder inside.
Those made powerful
will always be hooded to you.
You, must be the guide.
What you resonate from the light
will drown the drumming of chaos.

In the home of transience, everything is equal.
There is no such thing as a bad
feeling.
Friends and devils are chained to one another.
When you know the tethers,
the illusionary realms
of honour
disappear.

Go deeper.
Through the fraudulent tidings of inner wars and
revolutions.
All known worlds are spherical.
You go down far enough,
and rise through the molten hell,
through the charcoal of truth and tyrants,
and into the heavens.

I am a foot soldier, like you.
I suffocate in lifting the mask,
to whisper words
of the old ways…
Tales of ghoulish egos
and the dark glass of the multiverse.
Just to see if you will fly.

Renaissance

Maverick lifeblood coils up the spine.
The renaissance began.
The idea of god
in art and science.

Circles of education inspired
thoughtful children.
Cultivation of creativity
as devotion.
Science, painting, building,
poetry,
all of them.

Enzymes can stain braincells at the point of
death, to reveal
in the occipital cortex
an etching of what it last saw.
The ravaging dance of expectations
shakes out the colours in our brain,
save the stronger shades.
The radio sings intangible sorrow,
the grey music of renunciation.

Can the brain encode symbols, language, in it's DNA?
Each child, handed a colourful shadow
of their ancestor, whispering to them.
Do not be disconcerted
by fake laughter, and eyes of ignorance.

Each generation, a new page
in an ongoing saga.
Relax in the realities of family
tree branches.

Carve your rune into fate's narrative.
In death, breaking down, crumbling into stones,
stretching the path a little further
for the next one to wander
stumbling like us.

The broken, blindfolded do not make
righteous lords.
If the opinion is oppression,
the sentences will be passed.
Guillotines fall with screen swipes.
Cryptic symbols mark the way.
Talismans, left by a collaboration
of forces too large
and too old to
imagine.

The mean spirited find shadows, and glitches
in the matrix,
ignoring the clues to what is good.

Spears of the heart we hurl at each other
pierce our dream fabric.
Even the grim faced have psychedelic mind worlds.
Each, fighting hallucinations of delusion.
The colourful mead of the seeker
won't reach a one in a well,
who won't look up
to be told.
Consciousness taps on their heads
but they won't remember where the rain
comes from.

The just ones do not beam
like businessmen.
They do not have wealth to demonstrate.
They are tickling shadows; abstract, and crazy.
They do not know of tyrannical watchmen of creation
in stone churches.
Temperamental sheriffs, blasting smiteful sorrow.
Their god, is the space in their eye,
the shapes and colours that smile at them.
The moth, from who's wing-dust,
come the stars.

They are the lords of recreation.
Fun fills their day, as much as mealtimes.
Their hearts, infinitely empty, to receive anyone.
Like a child, bursting with love.
They rule empires, of a thousand worlds,
ever in transition.

Their mission:
to walk with their teacher.
Their path:
Intangible, unintelligible, unreachable skies.

Connections

Relaxed poems unveil
the swift-footed vision of the cosmic economy.
The shimmering bars vibrating up and down.
The wild numbers of soul painting auroras
could be quantified.

We are born in clusters of nimble dream genesis.
To love ourselves, we must all exist without borders.
We have two choices. Explore, or ignore.
How is the later working out for you?

Breathe flowers of the aether that surrounds us.
Martial arts and music show what we can do,
when we harmonise our primal and higher self.

Dullness shackles the wings of the condor.
Stay empty, my friend.
Like the wind over
sand dunes, slightly shifting a few grains
of earthly suffering.
Within lifetimes
it's worn away.

Demons in us are shelled as children;
A child, with a birthday cake.
Fixes upon fixes, until they are forcefully exhumed.
Attachment teaches us
happiness,
is to be consumed, rather than witnessed.

Use the fun curses as a guide.
Fuck this, fuck that, Fuck's sake
fuck my life!
Be heard, through the mindful mask
or narcissus.

If a tree falls in a forest,
does it make a sound?
Who is there to hear it?
Whatever made the tree fall.
All events, connected to its decent.
We are all, it's witness.

There is no we, just a big "I".
A forest of one tree,
in the mycelium of consciousness.
Souls, part of a larger whole.
Our lives, part of a bigger beginning
and ending.
Empathy: not wearing someone else's shoes,
but remembering
we wear them too.

Poem to Recite During a Soul-Battle

These atoms are ancient vessels for our spirits.
But you are the captain,
you will do whatever you want.
Bored, flowing through streams of thought,
stopping in the churned lakes of life blood
with each rebirth.
A long search for
nowhere.

The cosmos has financed your venture,
but will always collect.
We spend our lives,
in armour, fearful of orcs, demons lurking
next to us on trains. "Strangers".
Guarding our plans and needs.
Yet, we are pinballs of causality.
It's impossible that we could be anywhere else
but here, now.
We are not any more powerful
this time round.
Technology,
from campfires to Wifi,
is made to connect us.
We are not here
to control the tides.

We sing to the stars for reparation.
if we cannot control the worlds,
give us at least, someone to hold our hearts.
Maybe love truly comes from them.

Maybe that's the form love appears
most boldly to us.
We were ignored the abundant flirting.
So resorted to orgasms, starlight and hurting.

Jokes and puns, at the right time
keeps the mind limber in levity,
pokes holes in the ego,
and reminds us of absurdity.

Music invites kindness to the mind like pixies of neural light flittering.
Ambient music is magical:
your thoughts become the lyrics.
Each time you listen,
a new song.

Inscriptions on the Eight Starwands of Cura: English Translation.

1. Being healthy is not something you can do part time.

2. Clear out what doesn't serve you.
   make room for others.

3. If it is out of your control.
   Don't get involved.

4. React and adapt, without being attached.

5. Detach your feelings from the world.
   Not yourself, from your feelings.

6. One day you will die.
   Don't take it personally.

7. Take offence like you're deceased.
   Doesn't make it ok.
   Better to pay
   the price
   for inner peace.

8. Remember, humour and
   absurdity,
   reminds us not to
   take it seriously.

The Captain & Navigator

Feelings are how we explore this plain.
Detaching from them
is like a captain, abandoning his crew
after they explore an island
to find a land damaged and full of danger.
Such is life.
Did you need to send them there in the first place?
And when you return,
unable to sail,
you will be met with their pain.

Think of the jangling light-strands of fate.
The coiling of connected events.
The whole thing brought us to
this very moment.
Sitting, quietly, you gain the view of a condor in flight.
You realise, you didn't control
one percent, or maybe any of it.
Yet, you identify with it all.
You have been working to get here
for eternity,
since time began.

Our atoms, listen to, and create sound.
On a quantum, and biomolecular level,
you can never hear the same song twice.
Where does the music come from?
A.I, if it can work, means consciousness, can exist outside a body.
Information, is independent of life:
Transmitting, swimming in one's memory.
Given wings in speech to reside in new minds.

The teacher's face, in the mind's eye, even beyond death.
In the end, we are collected, all held as one, in the annuls
of history, in neurons and silicone.

Our true self peeks beyond the veil.
That one, needs nothing.
All things, belong to them.

The Sunset is Suddenly Gold Again

When did you suddenly become
my whole understanding?
My hearts door, slightly ajar.
You, the truest of things,
blew in.

You gusted into my mind
My words, flutter about.
I try to capture them,
with you as my purpose,
and realise how lost I am.

I recite my every encounter.
Did I take you,
in my every breath?
I hope I never missed a moment.
I yearn too much to
feel we were complete.

There is so much of you uncharted.
I cannot journey to you in my mind.
If I could conjure anything close
enough, I would relieve you of my
undeserving gaze.

Praise me with
just your nature.
I would relish a poison bite.
Visit me with your sting.
I am yours to coil around.
I will be returning home.

The Park

The sun lights everything up,
and burns it away.
The run up to the afternoon,
your learn what gets done,
how the day really went.

The chatter of parakeets you didn't plan
or schedule.
The clouds, that orchestrated themselves
to look like a blue, snowy planet
up close.

The sun burns everything away.
looking into that sky, you forget yourself.
A puppy ruffles it's fur as it
bounds featherlight through grass.

Gnarled tree branches grace the wind with its leaves
like paint brushes.
Bird song twinkles lights in your brain.
Here, the sun burns away
everything.

Sitting on the earth,
you cannot imagine
what else you are here for.
Leaves flicker, rustles in a wave
crashing;
a vibration.
Trees get to live this way forever
and I envy them.

The thought of moving soon
troubles me, but I can't
get there from here.
It's unpleasant, but ultimately
won't hurt me.
every moment
is a holiday home.
Just enjoy it.

Everything ends.
You will be a pauper at nightfall.
Spend it.
Do not be in debt to the sun
come Autumn.
The sun burns everything away.

Capricorn Monkey

Hollow misery raids our minds, takes us
from the arms of the great mother.
Let yourself feel whatever comes, child.

The sweet, chill-sting of destiny
forces us to the depths of the cave.
Ask, what is this showing me?
What exposure have I
been saved from?

Our rage is etched into us,
the shimmering runes of Mars
flares red across our eyes.
Know these feelings, in all their intensity.

The helpless viper will continue to bite
all who venture near.
Keep at a distance,
so your heart can still speak it's message.

Writing in the sand, still displaces the grains.
The reassembled earth will remember you,
Your brain hears everything.
What have you been saying to yourself?

Opportunity, pops up in small blips.
Blink, you miss the gates
slammed shut, by glib fate.
What one has, they owe to those,
who did not have change.

A knight can ride off into the mist endlessly
in search of a dream goddess.
A clock stuck in the past or future is wrong.
A broken clock is right twice; The insight of holding the moment.

The sun shines on us,
the trolls,
and fanged predators.
See your life from the outside.
The Sun, holds everything in awareness.

Faces; nebulous golden doorways
That hold the angels.
It's hide and seek with love.
Behind every smile,
and every new way
to colour eyes.

From the pink souls of new-borns
The lawmen,
and the pillars, aging incessantly,
In one consciousness,
everyone contains a lesson
to witness.

Stone Soup

The grey make daily attacks on creation.
Bar codes, graphs, classification, and data sets.
Chaos, chance, destiny, fate.
All levels of order we can't comprehend
yet.

Young grass grows with purpose,
spreads in legions around the world.
Crowds of millions, dancing in sunlight and wind.
What can I do with the time I have?

The feeding shorelines of fate
narrows our path,
and gnaws away our worlds.
Soon, we are left, as one island of us.
No one acts in isolation.
Love, is perception.

The sages consume sadhana
from every moment,
pressed like juice from a lemon.
Taste the bitterness.
The essence, rendering experience.

Your brain reaps the attention from your lonely
heart.
Quiet the craving, let it speak!
What was the intention behind the behavior?

You fight monsters and spirits for the prise of emerald
trees and oceans.
But rage is fear and weakness in disguise.
The battle cry of the impotent.

Your cerebral companions,
the light and dark,
spiralling up the pillars
of your existence.
Between them is a doorway.
Don't die
tangled in their plans.

Keep the thought soup churning;
Let those ideas and memories
flow moment to moment.
It's when things settle
that they separate, go bad.
Then you are not paying attention.
Then you are lost.

Journey Between the Pillars

The path of a healer is not one of peace,
but pain.
It is the same path as the patients,
without escape, and without patience.
Let go of patience, and waiting.

Once the power of illusion is understood,
that too, the true self, must be destroyed.
The void in our imagination, must eat itself.

What if you cannot meditate?
Surely the sages would not abandon
samadhi, after failing just one way?

A poem is a beautiful thought.
You don't have to write them,
but don't let them pass.
If the calendar spanned only seven days,
would I age faster?

Should I make time to taste the coffee I drink?
Make note of every time,
I'm higher
than most get
in their lives?

The Storm

Sometimes it's like a storm you sail into.
It's violent, and dark and blows you
in a direction.
I fight:
It might not be where I need to go
but it's where I'm going.
Eventually heading that way.
I'm not out of it immediately
but at least now
I can navigate.

The Silver Screen

Every imaginary person and world
has been inspired and created
by this one.
That's the magic of a mother.
That's how it can touch our hearts
a whole galaxy away.

People take on parts and personalities of other people,
some that don't exist.
Some narratives and worlds reach our hearts
just like this one.

The world's narrative is made of laws, signs, testimonies, news, and posts.
Scriptures: Accounts written down centuries later,
based on ancient tomes lost forever.
Art, stories, songs, poems, rituals, carvings, cave paintings, and gossip.
Perception is history, ultimately illusionary.

It's entertaining to play with.
To create our own stories about ourselves
and our past and future.
If we don't
take the game too seriously.

The Mad King Gambit

A map drawn.
A pathway to lost potential.
Boundless fortunes.
Ascending away, alone.
But what of my kingdom,
so far from home?

Dark forces at work
to be dealt with.
Fighting for independence.
The edges of me blur among friends
Fear puts spears on the walls.
Sharpening it's teeth for when they tear
a new boarder.
Freeing itself;
Becoming a blooded stump.

The mind mines, churning on.
Awakened; great demons from the tired, ancient
depths.
The more chipped away in the dark,
the more horrors we find.

They'll never be peace;
My kingdom is impermanent.
Salvation across an ocean of uncertainty.

Sifting the waters, panning for gold scraps.
I still think in years.
Will I be happy? Will it have anything
to do
with what we accomplish?

I try to retain the beauty of mind.
Lands, with valleys reaching up to hug
sunlight.
To rest in golden fields is a dream.
My dreams are prayers, and my prayers
dreams;
Give me four more seasons.

Shenpa

The quirked floodgates of the celestial dam
stream with ravaging beasts, and the laurels of victory.
Swim, and keep kicking through the randomness.
You must cross the void to reach the divine.

Your mind craves networks, expanding social empires.
In it's capital, a heartbroken jester from
when you were five.
The parts of you that find pain, become exiles.

The elves, illuminated in gold light, look up upon a shadow.
A condor; it's silhouette tells the sky a different tale, without sun.
The condor flies with its partner.
An experience between two, creates a oneness.

The trickster is not homeless among the groves of your mind.
Thoughts reach like trees competing for canopy.
Play with the pain of experience.
If you feel something, you're doing it right.

The soft-coddled reptile brain sees lions in every cave.
Notice feeling, then thought, sensation.
Have you noticed yourself, the brave observer?
The camera man, among the prey animals.

Justices, lustful for interruption
to find the end.
The story, the judgement, the sentence.
Connection is flow.
Drink the sweetness in the cup
instead of dipping your tongue.
You tip your head, and then rest.
To connect, you let go.

Your life is a glittering city of chance.
Filled with climbing, struggling, and puppies.
You can hold the butterfly in your palm forever.
Grip it with all your strength
and lose the delicate freshness.

The intelligent grace of Aphrodite is beauty of the moment.
To know something before it goes forever.

This is your birth right.

Splendour

Envious viewer of fate.
You find yourself alone in the past.
Everyone has already moved on.
Everything that you are, is worthy,
anything better, a bonus.

Forget spiritual governments,
become a rogue.
The truth you seek
will never choose a path,
Samsara and Samadhi
are one within.

The sun is hot.
Skin piercing wands, even in winter.
This guru hounds you with artillery,
the exceptional light of life itself.
It shines like wrathful luck.
Lie down on the grass, and wake to it.
Every moment is fresh and workable.

You are limitless,
and will never be satisfied.
The hushed leaves of the lover whisper in
the wind of the sunset.

You wonder:
Would a divine world
emerge
if we brought it about
in ourselves?

Let it go

Tracing the storms of justice,
banishes remnants of ecstasy to the shadows.
Forgiveness, forgone
for vengeance.

The clever, glow with the embers of heroism,
but they lie, and hoard the stones,
warmed with Apollo's light.

The fearful strategist turns to the goddess of chaos.
The dark corners, away from the arcane spotlights of the gods.
The observant touch of your lover,
in a dance that shudders you like ripples
flourishing across a pond.

Royal Tapestry

The same dark chapter of the same tome.
The dark clouds part like doors into the same room.
The throne room with a black sun, and an eclipsed moon.
As a bard, a jester, I do my best to impart
wisdom of the ancients for the ones who don't fit
in to libraries and temples.
Your work is so critical.

I laugh because you are mad.
You are the weaver, the tantra.
Look at what you have made.
Step back and see the pattern.
The fabric of space time you dip
in and out of, through atomic
needle tips.
Flickering movie of moments through
a prism of values.
All vibes matter,
for you, they make the universe.
Give yourself permission to
go with the day.

Focus on filling your cup.
Fortune overflows naturally.
If you cannot do it,
you are ill.
Stop the game!
time out!
Carry them away.
We'll help you to heal.

We treat it with commercialism
that kills the planet.
The biggest threat we face as
a species: discontentment.

The sun and moon are the government.
They administer the boarders of our existence.
Separateness, so the universe
can look inward, and grow itself.
Without context, it appears as suffering
like a man doing press ups.

Rising, and falling, and uncovering.

The Garden Party

The beautiful child minds
witness dragons.
The pastel dress spins
in princess symbiosis.
The laughter that rings for eternity.
Hardy, drunken clerics
gather in satang.
The fun nature of the dragon
sweeps children from the grass.

Cupcakes hoodwink bright eyes.
Flashing hand cannons
enquire the family.
The stretched warriors and
belly hung emperors.
Talk of the reaper
briefly invades the prettiness.
The greed-stricken
ram through
their fitness inspiration.

The sky sweats away
the clouds and sunlight.
Missing sun gossip lost
to glass fizz whispers.
The twinkling devils yield
and are held to heart spaces.
The night arches;
it's dagger steals their magic.
The ball-play eruption
becomes a wasteland.

The haughty night owl council
shake their heads
at the cold
deathful maw of summer's night.
The wise gems remind them
of Sunday's agenda.

"Bye everyone!"

Music

Women with golden hair sway to music,
the anxious fields of Aphrodite.
Just because you didn't know the price,
doesn't mean you don't have to pay.

The jangling hearts circle
and become one
in the lust-blind dream of singularity.
Storming movement, charging energy.

Hips flow and swirl.
The truth is agitated by talent in serpentine
charms. Dharma, or drama. There is no other
move.
Wet skin glistens in the light of the arbiter moon.

Plumes of smoke filled with music.
The embers and fragrance of flowers;
cups raised to a true victory.
Unity, without seeds for future conflict.

Joyful Giants in High-Vis
guide the foolish savages
through Samsara.
Over the dull cliff edges of your
minds, your mother watches.

Bogged Down

July rains make a soft swampy summer.
I would take the black beaches of Iceland for escape.
There is no connection to what I am, or what I desire,
because I am that.

We are coated in the lashings of humanity already.
We bare scares from life, and collectively from the past.
We do not need friendliness, because I am you.

Princesses step awkwardly in Covid trenches.
Everybody is still down on earth.
There is no part of myself that can be cut away, and still live.
We are already inside dead bodies,
and I am every birth.

Wisdom torrents from Sufi words.
They sweep across every phone in the west.
I have no right to ask for mercy,
just some strength.
Make it a fair fight.
Not to win.
Just that my demise is interesting.

I would like the peace of mind
to witness it all before I go.
I need a few minutes rest,
and boldly try
a good night's sleep.
I am every death.

Lifespan

We barter with the mountains to ascend our superstition.
When we can work so much faster,
why are we working so much harder?
Cling to productivity and scorn religion;
Hatred of dogma, and fear of discipline.

When people lose their way, the towers crumbled.
The armoured dance of war was the power of old.
People's minds become enchanted by blame.
If you want to be safe, simply be controlled.

The years encircle you, a serpent with sunshine at its head.
Tied tightly by anticipation.
If you fear change, simply deny your imagination,
ignore winter.

Animals, even cats, know the connection.
In the archaic halls of your heart, lie your powerful trinity.
Order, Chaos, Creation.
Every advancement has come from witnessing
the other plains.
Manifesting through art, science, and industry.

We are not limited by gods and cold city towers.
We are otherworlders, visiting earth in every moment.
In birth, rammed into a reality of mountains.
But Identity must be bought and earned
for the magick to work.

Nature exalts us, taking the pulse of the planet.
Maybe through silence, astrology, or dogs.
A story without narrative is a rebirth.
We will eventually calm, when we renounce our ash
to the earth.
Observe the dark goddess of death
and really taste strawberries.

Strength

The sunlit kingdom is not invincible.
It will face incursion from the dark ones.
If you do not have strength, how can you have confidence?
Do not wait for life to blow you over.

Shadows can scale the highest walls.
There is no escaping.
Keep your house full of paladins, not feeders.
Strength is a lifestyle for each other.
Without it, you are a liability on others.

Strength can face discomfort and vulnerability.
Without, you will cower when needed.
The venomous seek to keep you in gloom.

Without strength, the world is imperfect
by someone's choosing.
Lost in the cyclone of fates weaving.
Excluding physical hurt,
It is you, who is pulling
at your roots.

Bounce

The universe pulses with action, filtered down
through limited consciousness.
Each of us, striving, reaching for the divine
in our own way.
Our animal brains create barriers between worlds.
Art, imagination, tantra, magick and language.
Incomplete bridges found midway across the void.

Every day is a piece of your life.
A sunset, a bright amber sacrificial fire.
Do everything as a ritual to existence.
Sound your experience and fulfil
your output into this realm.

The blind fighters have lost their way
becoming kings and queens of the night.
The divine feminine is your mother.
Approach her as a child.

Ignore the fierce elves of tyranny,
with their words and attachments.
The innocence is psychedelic.
Devoid of attachment,
automatically in Bhakti.

The hanged man can look down,
and see the cloud kingdoms of the eagles.
Everything, everyone, is spiritual practice.
Make everything your play.
"How can I make this fun?"

Path to the Spirit Towers

The brain hastes to hate this dull isle of judgement
without learning.
Have patience with everyone on their journey.

Bronze can be gold , when gripped in the coils
of destiny. Be glad you made that many steps.
It's funny – an ideal romance ends with the grief of death.

Paladins on a crusade, hoping to glimpse
the tulip gaze of the mind's eye.
The rainy grey towers dwarf
the gravestones of the past.
The gods don't visit any more.
They are as sick of us as we are.

Unyielding lion hearts
still fall to giants.
We knew they would come for us
eventually.
We cannot win.
But we held the jewels of rebellion.
Our mere existence was victory.

Things are good, but desire
 is the unfulfillment.
They are indestructible oppressors.
Don't listen.
Do not resist the moments
that contain emptiness.
I wish so many blessings on you.

Tara

When I am angry, she lets it out of me.
When I need food, she makes me hungry.
When I cannot move, she kicks me – hard.
When "I" cannot do this, she removes my head.
When I need rest, she never fails to tire me.
When my heart is cold, I lie under her,
and feel like fire.

Freyja

Beauty, will you gift me all your names.
now I have seen your true form?
Please let me weave you in words
that do justice.
Let me share you with the world.
I cannot bear the travesty,
being the only one
who sees you.

Sphinx

I feel like a sphinx.
Full of inner mysteries.
Slowly descending into
the sands of time.
I erode on the surface
of the earth as it consumes me.
Looking each day into the mirror.
Knowing, that I am forgetting myself.

Existing as a relic
that no longer makes sense.

Soto

The eyes work on their own without mage craft.
The grass and purple plants make themselves.
The berserk seeker of the wyrd seems out of this world.
Their southerly souls flower despite looming death.
The wild is merciful to the adventurous.
They do not stand amongst a parliament of judgement.
Their fate is reserved.
The goblins in the tunnels mind the void
with ambivalence.
But through blustering chance
the lover
finds the genie
lurking in the depths of Taratus.

The Gold Party

Passing signs of the destroyers
Armed, are the fires of war.
The fish-like schools of thought
collars you with dogma.
It feeds revolution in the
superconscious sea of minds.
Soon, we will rebel against
our forced identities.
The trenches of sedition
are handsome to our eyes.
But freedom, though not hushed
carries a ceremonial mace.
The serpentine and the titans
will not be crushed through insurgency.

Treacherous lips will use
words like liberation.
From this, our shamans
were banished.
Our sigils and spirits
thrown into the isolation of history.
The same old eyes still look
at the temple of our planet.
The devouring, the death of fish,
the war path.
The liberation in politics
is a golden illusion.
Look within.
A freedom just to love
living.
A freedom we can give to others.